THE CANADIAN
ROYAL TOUR

THEIR ROYAL HIGHNESSES
THE PRINCE AND PRINCESS OF WALES

JUNE 14 - JULY 1
1983

TEXT: ROBERT JEFFREY and PAUL RUSSELL

 METHUEN

Toronto   New York   London   Sydney   Auckland

- ROYAL VISITS OF OTHER ERAS -

Although Canada has had a monarch as official head of state for almost 400 years, it wasn't until the late 18th century that an immediate member of the ruling Royal Family came for a visit. Up to that time, the French, then the British royal presence in our land, was merely symbolized by gifts...a statue of the Virgin from Louis XIV to the Church of Notre Dame in Montreal; silver urns from the Dauphin, son of Louis XV, to the Huron community at Lorette; altar silver at the chapel of the Mohawks at Brantford, presents to her allies from England's Queen Anne.

Then, in 1786, a Hanoverian prince, William (later William IV), came to Halifax as a naval captain. His father, George III, had just lost his "revolting" American colonies three years before. William would spend the next three summers based at the "Gibraltar of the North," acquiring a lusty reputation as sportsman, carouser and womanizer. He was especially fond of Frances Wentworth, the wife of John Wentworth, surveyor-general of the King's woods in North America. In 1791, when a grateful William had returned to Europe, he named John Wentworth governor of Nova Scotia.

But it seems that William was almost immediately replaced in Canada by another royal prince. It was his 23-year-old brother Edward who arrived at Quebec in 1791 at the head of a regiment of Royal Fusiliers. He also came, like William, not as a royal prince, but as an officer, on a tour of duty. He stayed for two seasons and seems to have developed a good rapport with the French-speaking population. War with the French Republic sent him to the West Indies in 1793, but when he returned to North America, this time to Halifax, he stayed until 1798 when an injury forced him back to England for proper medical care. While in Halifax, Edward lived with the beautiful Thérèse Bernadine Montgenêt, known as Julie, Madame de Saint-Laurent, whom he adored but was unable to marry, as she was a commoner. They particularly enjoyed their summers at a villa he had built on Bedford Basin where the prince and his friends would gather for concerts on summer evenings. In 1799 Edward was made commander of all British forces in North America. It is also claimed that the prince and Julie had a son while in Canada. The boy was raised as Robert Wood, by a royal servant, and grew up to take an active part in the lumber business of Lower Canada.

In 1802 Edward returned to Europe and took Mme Saint-Laurent with him. They remained together for almost twenty years until the need for an heir in the Royal Family compelled their separation, that he might marry Princess Mary Louisa Victoria of Saxe-Coburg-Gotha. The daughter of this marriage became Queen Victoria, who was probably never aware of her purported step-brother in Canada, Robert Wood. A "royal" would not return to Canada until the generation after Victoria.

The year is 1860, and royal tours, as we now know them in Canada, are about to begin. The visitor is no less than Edward, Prince of Wales, son of Queen Victoria and heir to the throne of the British Empire. As the United States, just south of the Great Lakes, open

Edward, Prince of Wales (Edward VII), visits Toronto during his 1860 tour.

The young Prince of Wales (Edward VIII) in the uniform of a Colonel in the Welsh Guards.

hostilities in their Civil War, Edward calmly dedicates Victoria Bridge, Montreal's new engineering marvel, and opens an exhibition of farm produce in Toronto. He travels on the new colonial trains, opens the new Parliament Buildings in Ottawa seven years before Confederation and rides a timber slide in Hull. He passes under numberless cedar-bough archways in numberless Canadian towns and proves a most popular guest. Canada remains fervently royalist.

In 1878 his sister Princess Louise came as wife of the Marquis of Lorne, Governor General until 1883. The Canadian government named a lake after her in the confederation's new national park at Banff. Their stay was a tenure, not a tour, but the royal couple did add a courtly air to Ottawa society, with skating parties on the pond at Rideau Hall, and the elegant pageantry of formal ceremonies on Parliament Hill. Louise's invitations and her royal presence were sought by all.

There were visits by other members of Victoria's large family. Prince Arthur came to hunt in Quebec in 1869. During his 1901 Canadian tour, while still a prince, George V recorded in his diary that he had shaken hands with 24,855 citizens.

It was not until 1919 that a new Prince of Wales, Edward's grandson, ventured across the Atlantic once more. His family had changed its name to Windsor, and the young Dominion that he came to visit had changed greatly in status, from the colony of 1860 to a 20th-century federal state, conscious of its recent contributions to the allied war effort. This was to be a visit of thanks for that effort. The young prince was "David" to his family and friends; his signature read "Edward P"; he would be Edward VIII in the history books. But that was far in the future in 1919.

In August of that year, the HMS *Renown* sailed out of Plymouth towards the Dominion of Canada, carrying the young Prince of Wales on the most important royal visit since that of his grandfather, over a half century earlier.

David was a dashing, fair-haired young man; everybody's idea of exactly what a British prince should look like. He was the model of correct dress, always pipe or cigarette in hand or mouth, always the good-natured casual air, hand in pocket, jaunty smile. He was the embodiment of youthful aspiration of his time; carefree, sophisticated, the playboy of the Western World. The reaction to him, in Canada, was tumultuous.

Thousands of Canadian soldiers had met or seen the prince while on duty during the war in Europe. They came out by the thousands to see him again, in large crowds in the principal cities, and in knots of a dozen or so at isolated rail crossings along the route of his private train. HRH touched every community in the country. In Toronto, he tried to shake hands with absolutely everybody who came to City Hall. After two hours of this it was apparent that he would not be able to finish, and he went out to the front steps to apologize to the thousands who were still waiting to touch the royal hand.

During his three-month stay, he fished in the Nipigon River; drove CPR #2231 from Flavelle to Thorold, Ontario; was named Chief Morning Star by the Stony Indians of Alberta; cut out a herd at Alberta's "Bar U" ranch; and laid the foundation stone of Parliament's new "Victory" (later to be called "Peace") Tower in Ottawa. If there had been any republican sentiment in the Canada of 1919, it was snuffed out by that visit. Canadians loved their prince.

David was back again in 1924. As he was loved by the people, he was lionized by the social set. He rode with the Toronto and Eglinton Hunt and had a "spill" while jumping a fence between the Mulock and Beverley Farms in Ontario's horse country. Despite the mishap, everyone on the hunt was unstinting in praise of the royal guest. One member of the party, Charles Morris, was quoted thus:

> He rides loose and well, and we could not lose him anywhere we went. He was always on my skirts, and I do think if he'd had better luck he could have overridden me many times, but he was too good a sportsman to do that.

In 1939 Canada greeted its first reigning monarch, David's brother, George VI, and his consort Elizabeth. There was some hostile reaction to this royal tour. Dr. Norman Bethune, Canada's great medical pioneer and future hero of the Chinese Revolution, was in Toronto at the time and wrote a letter to *The Toronto Star* criticizing the tour as a British propaganda move to draw an independent Canada into the looming European war. Propaganda or not, the new king and his lady were extremely popular as they travelled about the country. Canada's first limited access highway, from Toronto to Niagara Falls, the Queen Elizabeth Way, was dedicated by the royal couple before their return to England, and war. Fully meeting Dr. Bethune's predictions, Canada did proclaim a state of war with Germany in September of that year.

During the fifties, with the advent of safe commercial jetliner service, new generations of Windsors came to Canada a number of times. Elizabeth as a young nervous princess, then as a confident monarch. Margaret came to review troops. Charles to do the same. They came as a family to Expo 67, the Montreal Olympics and the Commonwealth Games in Edmonton. Prince Andrew came to school at Lakefield, Ontario. Charles visited Yellowknife in 1979 and Lester Pearson College on Vancouver Island in 1980. The Queen returned in 1982 to sign Canada's new Constitution.

But this royal tour of 1983 is a visit with a difference. This is a state visit by the Prince with his Princess, the future King and Queen of Canada. Charles is now a familiar "royal" in this country. It is his Princess who has centre stage on this occasion.

~ CHARLES AND DIANA ~
THE MODERN TRADITION

As they raise their family and take on more and more of the duties of royalty over the coming decade, Charles and Diana will be adding their own chapter to the unfolding saga of the modern British Royal Family. The role of the Crown will continue to change, as it has for centuries, to meet contemporary needs. This evolution of the monarchy is impelled by the expectations of the population at large and the expectations of the family that represents it.

The Windsors look back to Victoria as "Mater familias," and as modern as they may be, they still take their cue from that diminutive lady. From Victoria and her husband Albert, the modern royals acquired a heritage of dignity, propriety and responsibility, models of behav-iour that were lacking in the Hanoverian dynasty that came before. The adulation and wide respect enjoyed by the family today was not easily won.

Before Victoria, kings were often hissed and booed in the streets of London. On the occasion of George IV's death, *The Times* commented, "There never was an individual less regretted by his fellow creatures than this diseased King." Even Victoria was not beyond rude stories and jingles. But she worked hard to set an example, to become a role model of all that was considered proper, good and British. She gave the constitutional monarcy its new apolitical role...and a powerful mystique of awesome rightness of behaviour.

Throughout this century the Royal Family has been

ABOVE: *Charles takes his youngest brother Edward for a spin.*

RIGHT: *Diana at the Isle of Uist in Scotland's Western Isles in 1974.*

FACING PAGE, LEFT: *Diana when she was still a teacher at the Young England Kindergarten in London's Pimlico district.*

FACING PAGE, ABOVE RIGHT: *Lady Diana Spencer typically dressed in open-necked shirt and small flower print to watch Prince Charles play polo at Tidworth.*

FACING PAGE, LOWER RIGHT: *Engaged and at Ascot, the deep frill was already a hallmark of Diana's style.*

aduaIly ridding itself of much of this formal mystique, nd moving closer to the people. The development of ralkabouts and regular television appearances have een a recent breakthrough, but the development of hotography began this process of familiarization four reigns ago. Until George V's time, people knew their king by his portrait etched on coin or stamp. His actual presence on a state occasion had the quality of a magic show. And, although George V permitted his picture to be taken, he never let a photographer within a radius of 25 feet of the royal person.

Queen Mary was the first to make an effort to draw closer to her people in a humanistic, sympathetic way. She decided to enter shops, to make purchases just like everyone else. Before this startling innovation everything had been sent to the Palace for royal approval.

George VI and his consort Elizabeth were brought even closer to their people by the adversities of war. The king and his queen stayed at Buckingham Palace, al-though it would have been safer to move to the country. Their home was bombed, as were the homes of thousands of others. It would never have occurred to George V to move about bombed areas of London in World War I as his son George VI would do so frequently in World War II. As a result, when the war was over, George VI had become the very symbol of the indomitability of his people and Commonwealth. According to many opinion polls, his wife Elizabeth, now the Queen Mother, is still the most popular member of the British Royal Family.

Queen Elizabeth has extended this familiarization not only in Great Britain but throughout the Commonwealth and the world. She has toured the world more than any previous British monarch. She has been seen personally by millions of her subjects. She is the world's most photographed woman. Through the several books that have been published about her, she has become familiar in the most detailed way from her favourite

5

treats (strawberries mashed with sugar and cream) to her favourite pastimes (she loves jigsaw puzzles).

She has ensured that her children will be well known to her Commonwealth subjects by schooling them around the world—Charles in Australia, Andrew in Canada and Australia.

In the manner of their parenting, Charles and Diana have already taken this evolution of monarchy a step further by taking nine-month-old William with them on a three-week tour of Australia. Queen Elizabeth had suffered long separations from her children when they were very young, and it seems that Diana is not prepared to suffer in the same way.

Diana, in her very presence, has already altered the image of British royalty still further. She is a mother and Princess at the ripe old age of 22. She is also a dazzling beauty. Since her engagement became official in 1981, this young woman has taken the world by storm, dressing in her unique way, handling formal occasions with a freshness and a sense of humor that rivals her father-in-law in his younger days.

LEFT: *Charles and Diana arrive with Prince William for the start of their 1983 Australian Tour.*

BELOW: *The first family portrait.*

Diana's specialty is her natural spontaneity. At her first public appearance as Princess of Wales, in Cardiff, she spoke a few words in Welsh, then turned to Charles as if to say, "Was that all right?" She reminds people of the Queen Mother the way she spots the shyest child in the crowd, but teases the more bold. On her wedding day she was first to notice the crowd roaring for a kiss. The Prince carried through, but he asked his mother first.

Like Prince Bertie, who visited Canada over a century ago, and his wife Alexandra, Charles and Diana have long years as understudies to look forward to before the monarchy overtakes them. They will take this time to amply develop their unique representation of the British Crown and carry this proud institution into the 21st century.

ABOVE: *Wedding day on the balcony at Buckingham Palace.*

LEFT: *The royal couple leaving Gibraltar to begin their honeymoon cruise.*

~ THE ARRIVAL ~
HALIFAX AND THE NOVA SCOTIA TOUR

It's 12:30 p.m. ADT, June 14, 1983, and as the Canadian Forces Boeing 707 touches down in the sunlight, TRH The Prince and Princess of Wales are about to begin their state visit to Canada.

After months of planning, all was ready. Itineraries had been printed and distributed. The Royal Yacht *Britannia*, comfortable home away from home for all members of the Royal Family, was waiting in the harbour. It seemed that all of Halifax had been cleaned and pressed for the occasion.

When the royal pair appeared at the front door of the jet, the Royal Standard flying above them, cheers and applause erupted from the crowd. Batches of schoolchildren were instantly enchanted by this fairy-tale vision of a princess, with blue eyes, radiant smile and blonde hair, that appeared before them wrapped in a red and white dress with a red-ribbon-of-a-hat perched on her head.

Her prince was beside her, tanned and smiling, trim and polite. After a wave to all, they descended the staircase to be greeted by a waiting Governor General and Mrs. Schreyer.

Then began the first delay in a hectic and tight 18-day tour, the kind of delay that was to delight thousands of people across the country, for Charles and Diana stretched their planned walkabout by at least 20 minutes, and every time they repeated this on the tour, it meant that hundreds more got the chance to say hello. Diana, the Princess of Wales, was quickly engulfed by children. Her ribbon-hatted head would be seen among them, then disappear again as she stooped down to smile and take the hand of a happy little well-wisher.

Leaving their welcomers at Shearwater completely enchanted, the royal pair then disappeared into a closed limousine, only to reappear some 20 minutes later on the Garrison Grounds of downtown Halifax for the official welcome of the people of Canada, to be made by the Governor General. He spoke briefly about the Royal Family's long association with Halifax and closed with a welcome in Gaelic, in honour of the Prince's Welsh title.

Charles was not scheduled to speak here. Perhaps he was moved by the splendid weather, the enthusiasm or the sheer size of the crowd (an estimated 12,000). But speak he did, of his past association with Halifax, in his youth as a sailor, and of his feelings that this time and place were a most fortunate situation for the introduction of his wife to Canada and Canadians. His comments were met with an enthusiastic, almost hysterical response, and another lengthy walkabout began. This time the Prince and Princess would meet Canadian war veterans splendid in their medals and decorations, and groups of senior citizens not wanting to miss one more royal visit. And everywhere, there were the entranced children.

As the tour progressed, Diana proved to be a lively morning person, always radiant, no matter how early the occasion...and there were several early starts. A day's events generally ended by ten in the evening; no late-night whirls for this royal pair.

The next morning, in Halifax Common, thousands more had been waiting for hours for a glimpse of the future King and Queen of Canada. People were tired but excited with anticipation of a real-life glimpse of the new Princess of Wales.

"What do you think she'll be wearing?" reporter Sally Armstrong asked a fascinated nine-year-old.

"I don't know but I've never seen a royal raincoat," replied Lindsay Cameron. And well she might have expected to see one, for the rain and drizzle had started and had not let up.

But Charles and Diana were undaunted by the rain. The 21-year-old Princess appeared in a light beige summer suit and matching hat, unprotected by umbrella or expected raincoat. It was just after 11 a.m., and they had

FACING PAGE: *Charles and Diana arrive at Canadian Forces Base Shearwater, Nova Scotia to begin their 18-day visit to Canada.*

RIGHT: *The Governor General with Mrs. Schreyer takes protective action as the Canadian Forces aircraft rolls to a stop.*

already unveiled a plaque at HMC Dockyard and in-
spected a restored St. George's Church, designed in 1800
by the Duke of Kent, Charles' Great Great Great Great
Grandfather, before this reception and treeplanting ceremony on the common.

Their arrival in an open jeep drew waves of applause
and cheering, and the release of thousands of balloons.
One seasoned British reporter, a royal tour veteran,
commented that he had never seen such a reception for
Diana. It approached the hysteria usually reserved for
teenage rock stars. The recent tour to Australia had
received enthusiastic response, but nothing like this.

At the Hotel Nova Scotian the royal party and Haligo-
nian admirers were guests of Prime Minister Pierre Trudeau at a gala dinner and reception. The Prime Minister
talked with the crowds outside the hotel as they awaited
the guests of honour; it was rather like a warm-up act
before the big number. When Charles and Diana arrived, the crowds gasped in approval of her brilliant
white ball gown and glittering tiara.

The third and final day of the Nova Scotia tour was
spent in the towns along the province's picturesque
south shore. The Yacht took them to Shelburne Wednesday night.

Shelburne was settled by Loyalists 200 years ago, and
residents were celebrating this bi-centennial visit in period costume, with their town crier, in the restored
village square beneath a fluttering Union Jack of George
III's reign. There was an unhurried holiday mood as
Charles and Diana talked with children about their
18th-century hoops and dolls. In fact the Princess Diana,
red-suited in a long jacket, pencil-type skirt and black
Spanish-style hat, was clearly having such a wonderful
time talking to the children that a dutiful Charles appar-
ently found it necessary to cross the grounds to give a
gentle tug at her sleeve, a suggestion that she might press
on.

At Bridgewater thousands more waited in the emerg-
ing sunshine at the Parkview Education Centre as the
motorcade arrived for luncheon. In the large school hall
the 650 guests clapped in rhythm as the royal couple was
piped in to the head table.

They dined with Premier and Mrs. Buchanan on south
shore fare, fresh Nova Scotia lobster with cucumber and
tomato salad. Invited guests awaited anxiously to see if
Charles and Diana would don their long cotton lobster
bibs. Charles accepted his, Diana twice declined.

At Lunenburg there was a brief signing of the civic
register at Town Hall, and a bouquet of Lupin and
Broom from an anonymous admirer for Diana. Then,
back to HMY *Britannia* at Shelburne for the overnight
passage to New Brunswick.

The Nova Scotia tour introduced Maritime fog and
Maritime hospitality to the royal couple. New Brunswick
would emphasize both when Saint John, the fog-bound
Loyalist city, burst its seams with an exuberant outburst
of "Dimania," unmatched in the staid city's 200-year
history.

TOP ABOVE: *HMY* Britannia *breaks through the heavy morning
fog on its approach to Shelburne harbour.*

ABOVE: *Two admirers in broad-brimmed millinery attract the
attention of the Princess in the Shelburne village square.*

RIGHT: *Charles and Diana accompanied by the Governor General and the Deputy Prime Minister, Allan J. MacEachen.*

BELOW: *Prince Charles signs the Province of Nova Scotia guest book as Premier John Buchanan observes.*

RIGHT: *The Princess of Wales accepts roses from an elderly woman waiting to see her in Halifax.*

BELOW: *Their Royal Highnesses proceed slowly through the Halifax Common on the rainy second day of their visit.*

FACING PAGE, ABOVE: *The royal couple greet well wishers assembled in the Garrison Grounds, Halifax.*

FACING PAGE, BELOW: *Members of the Royal Canadian Legion await their opportunity to greet Charles and Diana.*

It became a symbol of the tour, HMY *Britannia*, banners flying in regal splendour, breaking through the dawn mist as it approached another Maritime port. The Yacht eased up to her berth at the foot of Saint John's Market Slip at 6:30 a.m., on Friday, June 17, 1983, bringing Charles and Diana to New Brunswick. People had already begun to gather, despite the fog, in this beautifully restored historic area of the Saint John waterfront.

By 9:45 a.m., when TRH disembarked from *Britannia*, the red-bricked enclave was jammed with excited citizens. The mood was jubilant. They cheered Diana; they cheered the Prince; and the mayor, Elsie Wayne; and the Premier, Richard Hatfield; and the Lieutenant-Governor, George Stanley; and every individual blast of the 21-gun salute. When Charles responded by telling all how pleased he was to be in "St. John's," they even applauded this typical but rarely appreciated mispronunciation of their home town's name.

As the walkabout began, the fog cleared, assuring 55,000 people that they would indeed catch a glimpse of these royal celebrities. Children pressed the security lines as the pair walked and talked. Diana would turn to smile in one direction, shake hands in another, all with a clearly growing confidence. By now, the fourth day of their tour, she was noticeably more comfortable, more at ease with her new Canadian admirers. The walkabout went beyond the scheduled time but was still to be cut short of the planned circuit, because of genuine concern that someone might be hurt in this unexpectedly large press of exuberant fans.

Charles and Diana then motored slowly up King Street to the Loyalist Burial Grounds, and the Prince laid a wreath in honour of the founding fathers resting there while the present generation of teenage descendants clicked cameras from precarious perches in the tree branches overhead.

In the nearby white clapboard and lilac-gardened community of Rothesay, 5,000 schoolchildren lined a playing field at Rothesay Collegiate, waiting to sing, dance, play instruments and tell stories to honour the royal guests. TRH drove through the throng in an open jeep, then walked among the children. A band piped up the Beatle song *Yellow Submarine* as Diana, in a soft yellow suit and matching hat, extended her ungloved hand to these eager young New Brunswickers.

As TRH had come a long way to see them, many people made special efforts to reciprocate. One family from the Annapolis Valley in Nova Scotia was so disappointed when Charles' visit there was cancelled, they drove on to Bridgewater to catch up. The Prince had just left. Two misses; one last try. The determined family drove out of province to Saint John where their effort was met with success. During the walkabout in Market

Square, they were fortunate to be at the front of the crowd. The entire family shook hands with both Charles and Diana.

The "Dimania" of New Brunswick extended right up the province's social ladder. That evening Premier Hatfield toasted the royal couple at a state banquet held in the new Saint John Convention Centre. Mr. Hatfield was awestruck. He talked of the fires of love and left Charles, who rose to respond, "speechless." Later, when Mr. Hatfield was queried by the press on his extravagant phrasing, even asked if perhaps he had taken too much wine, he replied that indeed he had been "drunk, totally drunk on her charm."

Saturday, the second day of the New Brunswick tour, saw TRH in the northern reaches of the province, where the largely francophone population often greeted them in French and was obviously thrilled when the Prince replied in the same language. At Charlo Airport, just outside Campbellton, on the Quebec border, Micmac children dressed in buckskin performed a snake dance to welcome the royal couple to this forested land of salmon fisheries and paper mills. After the dance came gifts with

ABOVE: *At St. Andrews Charles is surrounded by latter-day Loyalists, some decked out in period costume.*

FACING PAGE, TOP: *The Princess talks with Archdeacon Nathais Jones after Sunday service at All Saints Anglican Church.*

FACING PAGE, LEFT: *Diana shakes hands with sea "cadettes."*

FACING PAGE, RIGHT: *A well-placed fan catches the eye of a smiling Charles.*

ABOVE: *Straddling his father's shoulders, a youngster greets Prince Charles in Market Square while Mayor Elsie Wayne chats in the background.*

TOP ABOVE: *A dutiful cadet stands at attention as Charles shakes hands at Rothesay.*

a homespun touch, mittens for Charles and Diana and moccasins for their son, Prince William.

At Sugarloaf Provincial Park they stopped for luncheon beneath a yellow-striped awning while crowds gathered on the slope of a nearby ski-hill. This was a casual get-together; the Princess wore a broad-rimmed straw hat, the Prince was in loafers. In Campbellton itself, Charles talked with the mayor, signed the town visitors' book and spoke of his pleasure in celebrating the community's 25th anniversary.

In nearby Dalhousie, the grade one students from L.E. Reinsborough Elementary School presented their dramatic version of the Cinderella story. The style of the young thespians was most artful. Crinkled noses expressed the nastiness of the ugly sisters; a sigh, or a hand on the heart, suggested the rapture of the Prince and Cinderella. Sheer wonder animated their performance, for the children thought that the tale had come true. Prince Charming and Cinderella were there with them for one magical afternoon in this small community on the Bay of Chaleur.

It was Fathers' Day, Sunday, June 19, in St. Andrews-by-the-Sea as HMY *Britannia* anchored offshore at New Brunswick's southerly tip. Charles and Diana arrived at dockside by launch. They motored slowly up King Street, passed the elegant frame architecture of this handsome Loyalist town, to All Saints Anglican Church, a white clapboard towered building surrounded by majestic elms. There they worshipped with the regular parishioners, carrying on a simple everyday Sunday routine of church service and conversation with the rector, followed by lunch. What made this typical activity unusual was the crowd of 7,000 people that had gathered under the elms just to watch.

THE CENTREFOLD PICTURES

FACING PAGE 16: *Prime Minister Trudeau greets TRH on their arrival at the Hotel Nova Scotian for a state banquet.*

CENTRE OPENING, LEFT: *Diana is radiant in shocking pink.*

CENTRE OPENING, RIGHT: *A dashing Prince of Wales meets guests at Rideau Hall.*

FAR LEFT, ABOVE: *Premier Lougheed welcomes Charles and Diana on the steps of the Alberta Legislative Building.*

FAR LEFT, BELOW: *HMY Britannia at anchor under watchful RCMP guard.*

CENTRE: *The nation welcomes the Prince and Princess of Wales with pomp and circumstance in the shadow of the Peace Tower on Ottawa's Parliament Hill.*

FAR RIGHT, ABOVE: *The stark majesty of a giant iceberg framed by passing royal pennants offshore from Newfoundland.*

FAR RIGHT, BELOW: *Red tunics and a brass band in Ottawa.*

FACING PAGE 17: *Diana gives Canadians a sampling of her trend-setting taste in millinery.*

The pomp and circumstance of the Canadian royal tour built to a crescendo in the nation's capital: there was a 21-gun salute, 100-man honour guard, a state banquet at Rideau Hall, a new version of *O Canada* performed by the RCMP band, and a commemorative medal struck by the Royal Canadian Mint.

The royal couple arrived at CFB Ottawa at three p.m. and drove slowly along Colonel By Drive to Parliament Hill where an estimated 40,000 people waited, many for over five hours in the 30 degree C. heat, to say hello to the future King and Queen of Canada.

The Governor General and Mrs. Schreyer were on hand to greet the arriving motorcade, and a snappy line of red uniforms and bearskin hats snapped to attention for the Prince's review.

Then, the now famous walkabout began. As the Prince and Princess turned to stroll up the red carpet towards the Peace Tower, the afternoon heat took its toll as perhaps half a dozen guardsmen fell forward like toy soldiers bumped off a shelf. Military support staff were on hand immediately to revive the weather's victims.

Diana, in a long-sleeved dress of blue, yellow and white stripes, white plumed hat and white pumps, met her most aggressive fans of the whole tour. They chanted her name as she moved up the walkway, they held forth signs of welcome and thrust bouquets of flowers towards her. At least two young women, Linda Olé, 17, of St. Lambert, Quebec, and Charlotte Bus, 16, of Orangeville, Ontario, natural look-alikes for Diana, were dressed in her style to emphasize the similarity. As she passed along the cheering lines and said hello, she left a trail of tears of excitement behind her. One red-headed young lad from Vermont extended his bouquet of flowers to the Princess and as she leaned to take it, he was so overcome by the moment that he just rose towards her and kissed Diana on the cheek. She gave him a smile in return, and the American teenager broke into tears.

At a reception on the dimly lit Gothic interior of Parliament, the legislators were as enthralled as the children outside, all pressing forward to meet the royal couple. Tactful RCMP officers kept the proceedings orderly.

The love-in on the Hill continued until about 5:30 when Charles and Diana left by car for Rideau Hall, the imposing vice-regal residence in Rockcliffe Park, their official Ottawa home. A private but very formal dinner was held that evening in their honour. The Governor General wore his Order Of Canada insignia; the stunning Diana wore a pink organza ball gown with tie-string straps topped by a diamond and pearl tiara.

But parliamentary procedure disrupted the banquet before it began. All of the formally attired politicians invited to the soirée left hurriedly by a side door as soon as they had passed along a receiving line, compelled to return to Parliament where a vote had been called on the controversial Crow's Nest Pass Rate Reform Bill. Prime Minister Trudeau, with a rose pinned to his white jacket, and House Speaker Jeanne Sauvé in décolletage led the rush by limousine to the House while ex-Tory leader Joe Clark entertained Diana at one table in the Rideau Hall ballroom and Maureen McTeer chatted with the Prince at another. By 9:30, the harried MPs were back at the banquet, and the guinea fowl feast commenced without further incident.

Tuesday morning Charles and Diana planted an oak tree on the lawns of Rideau Hall, carrying on a tradition started by visiting royals over a century ago. Then, in the entrance hall of the mansion, the Hon. Jean-Jacques Blais presented TRH with a medallion struck by the Royal Canadian Mint in honour of their visit.

At 11:30 a.m., the royal couple arrived at the new Ottawa police headquarters for an official welcome from the mayor of Ottawa, and the official opening of the new building, an honour delegated to Diana. It was also June 21st, and four youngsters representing the youth of Ottawa had gifts for Prince William, who was celebrating his first birthday back home in London.

The hot weather interrupted the schedule at the next rendezvous: a luncheon at the Chateau Laurier with the

A flashing smile from the Princess, and a meditative glance from Charles, in the gardens of Rideau Hall.

Ottawa Kiwanis Club. With all air conditioners operating at maximum levels, the power went off in downtown Ottawa, and although there was some emergency light at the Chateau, the air-conditioned salon quickly warmed up. Everything was back to normal by the time Charles rose to speak, making his first speech on a controversial subject on the tour. He spoke of the dangers of acid rain, not only in North America, but in Europe as well. He teased the Kiwanians by remarking that when he was first invited, he thought they were an Indian tribe, and he then added that perhaps native peoples have a better understanding of nature and man's place in it than we of the industrialized nations.

Charles and Diana then had the afternoon off to prepare for Prime Minister Trudeau's barbecue at Kingsmere Farm at seven in the evening. A guest list that had started at about 250 had swollen to 1200 by the time TRH arrived. The Prince was casually dressed in jacket and open shirt, Diana was her most casual during the tour—no hat. The Prime Minister was disarming in a cream-coloured Mexican summer shirt. Charles and Diana moved among financiers such as Conrad Black, actors and actresses such as Gordon Pinsent and Charmion King, hockey players including Lanny McDonald

FACING PAGE: *A radiant Prince and Princess are honoured at a state banquet hosted by the Governor General and Mrs. Schreyer at Rideau Hall.*

The Princess in the shadow of Rideau Hall.

ABOVE: *Charles and Diana honour a royal visit tradition by planting a tree at Rideau Hall.*

LEFT: *At Rideau Hall, the Hon. Jean-Jacques Blais presents TRH with a gold medallion struck to commemorate their visit to Canada.*

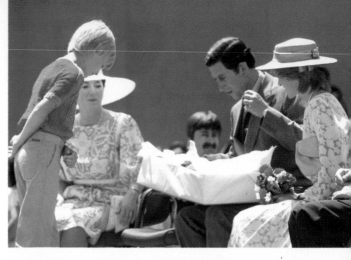

and Ken Dryden for about an hour, then sat to dinner on grilled Atlantic salmon, which they preferred to rib-eye steak, the other selection for the evening.

Wednesday morning the Ottawa sunshine and heat continued unabated as Charles and Diana arrived at the new Terry Fox Centre in east-end Ottawa to meet residents of this unique Canadian facility, where eligible students take courses in the study of their country's institutions. The Centre was furnished largely through a $250,000 cheque from the Royal Canadian Legion given as a wedding gift to the royal couple who then donated it to the Centre.

"It's nice to see a wedding present actually put to good use," Charles told dignitaries as he toured the building, then planted a tree. His brief speech praised the young Terry Fox, who ran halfway across the country with one artificial leg before succumbing to the cancer that finally killed him. He accomplished much, said the Prince, "despite his hideous handicap. We should all be inspired by his inner courage."

The heat was intense for the crowds waiting outside, their bouquets of wild flowers wilting in the midday sun. As Charles had talked throughout the tour of previous visits to Canada by his relatives and ancestors, many of the families that crowded the streets at every stop on the tour were also carrying on their own traditions. Mary Bush of Ottawa brought her four-year-old son Cameron

ABOVE LEFT: *A close-up look at Charles and Diana just before the official opening of Ottawa's new police headquarters.*

TOP ABOVE: *June 21 was Prince William's birthday, and the children of Ottawa gave his parents a gift to take back to London.*

ABOVE: *As Diana proudly looks on, an eloquent Charles stands to speak to members of the Kiwanis Club at a luncheon held at Ottawa's Chateau Laurier.*

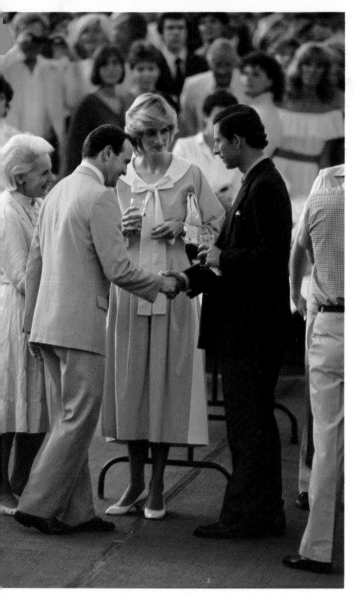

TOP LEFT: *In a casual mood, Prime Minister Trudeau welcomes TRH to Kingsmere Farm for a barbecue.*

TOP RIGHT: *Diana's now famous hair-style catches the late afternoon sunlight at Kingsmere.*

ABOVE: *The Prince and Princess are delightfully informal as they pass among the guests at Kingsmere. Mme Jeanne Sauvé, Speaker of the House of Commons, is making an introduction.*

OVERLEAF: *An affectionate gesture, rarely seen by the public, as TRH cruise down the Rideau Canal, waving farewell to Canada's capital.*

for a look, although she was sure that he thought Diana was Princess Leia from *Star Wars*. "This is an historic event," said Mrs. Bush. "I saw the Queen at Vineland Station when I was just little." She wanted similar royal memories for her son.

At the National Arts Centre TRH passed down the hillside to the Rideau Canal among a 5,000-strong crowd of fans as eager to see the Princess's fashions as to see Diana herself. One young man brandished a sign declaring: Look out Cheryl Tiegs, Here comes Diana.

Since Diana's fashion has caught so much world attention, the Palace is now getting requests for the clothes off her back. While the couple were in Ottawa, London received a request for a dress from the Princess's wardrobe for the annual celebrity auction and strawberry social of the Belton House and Teen Girls Home. The Palace said no. For no matter how worthy the cause, if a donation was made, future requests would be overwhelming.

When Diana reached the canal-side, everyone got a clear look at her round-necked turquoise silk dress and hat, accented with a single strand of pearls and pearl earrings. One ecstatic woman squealed, "O look at her hat." Another quipped, "She's in turquoise, so she'll look great on the canal!"

Diana smiled, waved and boarded the federal government yacht, *Rideau*, for a 25-minute cruise along Ottawa's inner-city waterway en route to their aircraft. On the rear deck of the yacht, the couple were joined by Environment Minister John Roberts, who may have been embarrassed by the unusually high level of algae in the water due to the heat wave, and Ottawa Liberal MP John Evans who was all smiles. Charles stood for a while with his arm around the Princess, giving photographers, on the following launch, the most relaxed, tender portrait of the couple they were to get on the entire tour.

At CFB Ottawa, Charles and Diana said farewell to their official hosts, the Governor General and Mrs. Schreyer, and Diana shook hands with the police motorcycle escort that had been with them for the past three days, waved to the crowds and boarded the plane that would take them from Ottawa's hot summer to the cool shore breezes of Newfoundland. . . a drop in temperature of 20 degrees C. in three and a half hours!

A bitterly cold wind blew across the tarmac, and a towering blue-green iceberg stood temporary sentinel at the entrance to St. John's harbour, as the Canadian Forces jet carrying the royal party arrived in Newfoundland on Wednesday afternoon, June 22.

When Diana emerged from the plane, she seemed as fragile as a spring bouquet, in her pink silk dress and jacket with matching hat, but she braved the elements like a trooper, elements that even caught Premier Brian Peckford shivering and pacing in his summer suit.

"Never mind the weather, it's the welcome that matters," Diana remarked while shaking hands with Penny Case, 17, of St. John's, one of several thousand who braved the chill in raincoats and parkas to welcome the Prince and Princess to a celebration of 400 years of close ties between Newfoundland and Britain.

Newfoundlanders had been looking forward to this party for months, and neither bone-chilling weather nor the rare IRA placard could dampen their enthusiasm. This visit was to have all the exuberance and fun of a family get-together, and the tone was set at the airport when the band finished the ceremonial salute, then dashed immediately into up-tempo *Squid Jiggin' Ground.*

The merriment followed the motorcade as it swept slowly into St. John's to a reception at Government House. Here Charles and Diana found shelter from the weather and a glowing welcome from assembled legislators and jurors in this classic Georgian building which had been the symbol of Newfoundland's British colonial status, before it joined Confederation in 1949. Then the obligatory tree had to be planted, and they returned once more to the Royal Yacht, in downtown St. John's. It was just after seven in the evening, but with the time lost in flying east from Ottawa, it had been, for Charles and Diana, a long day.

Thursday, June 23, was their first full day in Newfoundland, and the sun came out in greeting as Canadian naval divers from HMCS *Assiniboine* checked the hull of *Britannia.* The royal couple left the Yacht by 10 a.m. and crossed St. John's by slow motorcade to George V Park.

When Charles and Diana emerged from their limousine by Quidi Vidi Lake to open a province-wide "Festival of Youth," there were gasps and cheers from the 5,000 that had come, as others before them on this tour, to see their fairy tale come true. Diana, once more, stole the show in a red and white silk dress with three-quarter-length jacket and white hat.

Charles gave a brief speech, based on a few notes that he kept at hand, on the pride and problems, of being young, which he was more keenly aware of now that he was a father: "We do, as parents, realize the responsibility we now have towards one child at present, and I hope

several more in the future." The crowd cheered lustily, and Diana blushed and looked down at her red shoes.

Charles again reminded everyone that royalty can blunder on these occasions, just like ordinary folk. He said pointedly that he knew he was in St. John's and not Saint John, referring to his earlier confusion in a speech in the New Brunswick city where he had said he was happy to be in St. John's.

Charles and Diana then split on a walkabout inside nearby Memorial Stadium where they talked with young people gathered around the various displays set up for the youth festival.

Later in the morning they stopped at the Janeway Child Health Centre where they talked with young patients in the lobby before going on to visit the wards.

Diana took the afternoon off, resting on board *Britannia,* while Charles returned to George V Memorial Field to inspect a Royal Canadian Legion parade and to present new colours to the Royal Newfoundland Regiment. Charles looked every inch a soldier in the gold braid of his colonel-in-chief's uniform from the Lord Strathcona's Horse (Royal Canadian) Regiment as he

HMY Britannia at anchor in a foggy St. John's harbour.

reviewed the formation, then spoke briefly on New-foundland's significant contribution to the allied cause in two world wars. There was a half-hour military ceremony of presentation, two royal salutes and the pageantry was complete. At least three generations of fighting men were on the field together, honoured by the Prince of Wales.

The day was capped with an elegant state dinner at the Hotel Newfoundland where Diana, resplendent in a yellow gown and tiara, dazzled the 700 Newfoundland élite invited for the occasion. They dined on Newfoundland fare: cod, sirloin of beef and a concoction called "Bakeapple Britannia." Then Premier Peckford gave a brief synopsis of Newfoundland's long history. He talked of the province's new phase of economic growth, and spoke with pride of its heritage: "We are proud that some things have stayed and will stay the same. One of them, Your Royal Highness, is our abiding loyalty to the Crown."

Then came gifts for Charles and his family: duffle parkas for TRH and a snowsuit for Prince William. "We'll make a rather good team," mused Charles in his acknowledgement as he surveyed the matching outfits.

Newfoundland was the only province on the tour that the Prince had not visited, and he found it "nice to come to a place where neither of us has ever been before." He found the island fascinating, especially its place names and regretted that he and his wife could not visit them all, especially "Leading Tickles West," a reference that drew appreciative but very polite laughter from the assembled guests. Then a band played the *Ode to New-foundland*, and guests had a chance to talk personally with Charles and Diana in the Court Garden of the hotel.

Friday, June 24, was St. John's Day, an annual holiday in Newfoundland commemorating John Cabot's sighting of the island on that day in 1497. But this St. John's Day had added significance: the Prince and Princess arrived at Canada Games Park to inaugurate a province-wide celebration of the 400th anniversary of Sir Humphrey Gilbert's claim of the island for the British Crown in the summer of 1583. Newfoundland was Britain's first colony.

Again the weather co-operated, and the royal couple arrived in an open Rolls Royce, owned by Andrew Crosbie, brother of MP John Crosbie and driven by a scarlet-coated Mountie.

FACING PAGE, ABOVE: *Girl Guides get a rare close-up look at Diana's jewellery.*

FACING PAGE, BELOW: *A decorated Charles inspects the Royal Canadian Legion parade in St. John's King George V Memorial Field.*

LEFT, ABOVE: *Charles plants the seventh tree of the tour.*

LEFT: *Diana lends an ear to Newfoundland Premier Brian Peckford.*

An hour later they were in Cape Spear National Park, at the lighthouse which marks the most easterly point in all Canada. The view from the landmark is spectacular, but the fog had by then engulfed them and the crowd of 5,000 who had caught early buses to the park. "Like smoke from fire, it suddenly engulfed us," commented Hope Toumiskey to reporter Leslie Scrivener.

The royal motorcade returned to St. John's for official greetings from Mayor John Murphy and a civic luncheon. That evening Charles and Diana hosted a reception on board HMY *Britannia* and all watched the Beat Retreat Ceremony at 10 p.m.

Later, the Yacht quietly slipped her moorings and slid out of St. John's harbour during the night, headed for Conception Bay where TRH might experience the more typical Newfoundland way of life found in the fishing outports along the coast.

On Saturday, their last day on the island, with *Britannia* at anchor in the Bay that had been headquarters for 17th-century pirate Peter Easton, the royal couple visited the fishing villages at Carbonear and Harbour Grace. Carbonear's population swelled for the visit. Of its 5,000-strong population, 7,000 were on hand to greet Charles and Diana, including Nellie Carter, queen of the royalists, with a Union Jack sewn on her white summer purse. In Harbour Grace's St. Francis Field they met many in the local community and heard a brief concert of down-home "Newfie" folk songs.

By mid-afternoon, HMY *Britannia* was sailing out of the caplin-filled Bay while huge whales leaped gracefully as if in salute.

For the next 36 hours, the Yacht would remain at sea, bound across the Gulf of St. Lawrence for Charlottetown, Prince Edward Island. Charles and Diana would enjoy Sunday alone, but for the Yacht's complement of 256 men and 21 officers. What do a prince and princess do to relax? Perhaps they watch television like everyone else. A videocassette was rushed by taxi to the Yacht at the Prince's request just before it left St. John's harbour. The cassette was dispatched through the crowds and was taken safely on board. So we may assume that Charles and Diana spent their Sunday curled up on the Yacht watching *Tootsie*, while orders on the upper decks were given silently by signal or on a notice board, so as not to disturb the royal screening.

RIGHT: *A snappy Prince of Wales reviews his guard of honour.*

RIGHT, ABOVE: *Her tiara sparkling in the night, a golden Princess of Wales talks with guests at a state banquet in St. John's.*

~ PRINCE EDWARD ISLAND ~

Monday, June 27, and Charles and Diana are in the public eye once more as HMY *Britannia* enters Charlottetown harbour to the cheers of waiting crowds. Shortly after ten in the morning, they arrived at Province House, the stone Georgian Assembly House where the 1864 Charlottetown Conference spawned the national debates which led, three years later, to Confederation. Here they met with Premier James Lee, Mrs. Lee and the Speaker of the Assembly, Marion Reid and her husband, Mr. Lee Reid.

The later afternoon was a private time on the Yacht, time to prepare for an evening of music and lobster in the nearby town of Montague. June Hicken, manager of the Lobster Shanty North, a casual seaside motel and pub, had been cleaning and polishing for a month in anticipation of the evening's guests at this "down-home" buffet dinner hosted by W. Bennett Campbell, Federal Minister of Veteran's Affairs. But it was a casual evening with no red carpet. And that's how Ms Hicken wanted it. Nothing fancy; just good food. As for the preparations beforehand, she passed that off as just a "little tidying up."

RIGHT: *Charles signs a municipal guest book during the tour of Prince Edward Island.*

BELOW: *Diana chats with young P.E.I. fans in front of Charlottetown's Province House.*

Later that evening, HMY *Britannia* sailed along the coast to deposit its royal passengers at 10 a.m. on Tuesday morning, at the port of Summerside. TRH disembarked at the Summerside Yacht Club wharf to a relatively quiet, almost reverent reception, then travelled by motorcade to Memorial Park where they met World War I veterans, four mayors and manoeuvred a quick walkabout before moving on to Somerset Manor and an assembly of about 60 elderly residents who waited patiently in the dining hall, flags in hand, for the royal visitors. Diana and Charles were worth waiting for.

In the afternoon Lieutenant-Governor Joseph-Aubin Doiron and Mrs. Doiron hosted a grand reception for 1,600 invited guests on the lawns of Fanningbank, the vice-regal residence in Charlottetown. Here the Prince, gallantly determined to personally meet everyone, even shook the paw of Hooper, the seeing-eye dog of Kevin McGuigan, a public relations officer for the Canadian National Institute for the Blind. He shook McGuigan's hand too, very firmly.

Later that evening the royal couple hosted their final reception of the tour on board *Britannia*. They bade farewell to their crew and their "floating home away from home" the next morning before flying to Edmonton for the last stop on their whirlwind tour of Canada. *Britannia* lifted anchor later that morning heading out to the open Atlantic, and home.

LEFT: *An eager hand reaches through the crowd to greet the smiling Prince.*

BELOW: *TRH are serenaded by a military band at Fanningbank, the residence of Lieutenant-Governor Doiron.*

~ EDMONTON ~

At a dinner in the Hotel Nova Scotian at the beginning of the tour, Prime Minister Trudeau, in his opening remarks of welcome, had said that Maritimers were a "gentle, respectful people," but that Charles and Diana would find the West "the working part of the trip."

But if the Prime Minister felt that the Western reception for the royal couple would be less enthusiastic than the Eastern welcome, he was mistaken. Over 70,000 people lined the streets and squares of downtown Edmonton, despite the sometimes ankle-deep mud from recent heavy rains, to give Charles and Diana a hooting yahooing, whistling Western hello.

Premier Peter Lougheed waited on the legislature steps where Charles acknowledged the crowds and seemed genuinely proud that he and Diana were "Alberta's own royal couple." The Premier used this occasion to announce the formation of two annual scholarships in commemoration of the royal visit, scholarships that would send young Albertans to study at one of the United World Colleges, a favourite interest of Charles, instilled in him by his late uncle Lord Louis Mountbatten.

The biggest crowds were still to come, waiting for a mid-afternoon walkabout in downtown Sir Winston Churchill Square. It was a festive scene with banners flying from lamp-posts and people hanging out of office windows, waving placards and handkerchiefs at the royal couple below. The skyscraper-ringed square held at least 40,000 Edmontonians, cheering wildly as Charles and Diana arrived. There were chants of "We want Di," picking up on the chorus that was now familiar to reporters covering the tour. As Diana passed among the crowds, many people broke into spontaneous bursts of the *Happy Birthday* song, anticipating her 22nd birthday on July 1st.

About seven that evening Charles and Diana were back on view, resplendent in period costume especially designed for the event in London. Charles was garbed in the late 19th-century formal wear that his Great Great Grandfather Edward VII might have worn. Diana took his arm in a cream lace floor-length day dress of the 1870s. They were off to a barbecue with a difference. TRH and 800 others, all dressed to recreate the halicon days of the Klondike Gold Rush, would dine that evening on Alberta beef in the dramatic outdoor setting of the city's recreated 19th-century palisaded trading post, Fort Edmonton.

BELOW: *A provincial welcome on the steps of the Alberta legislature.*

RIGHT: *Diana displays her flair for fashion on her first day in Edmonton.*

Thursday morning, June 30, the royal couple were whisked off to Garneau Village, the sports complex housing the athletes preparing for competition in the World University Games. The young competitors from 98 nations around the world were clearly delighted with the royal couple. Most of them were about the same age as Diana. The banter was engaging and animated.

Sue Denton, 20, of Hamilton, gave the Prince and Princess each a pair of punk sunglasses—the narrow plastic wrap-around kind with a horizontal slit of dark glass. Charles tried his on immediately, causing the area to light up with flashing cameras. Diana carefully turned away to try hers on. No pictures please.

In the afternoon at the Jubilee Auditorium, Charles, looking suitably academic in long red robes, received an honorary degree from the University of Alberta, before an invited audience of 2,700 guests.

July 1st started badly. It was cool and drizzly with pockets of fog in the Saskatchewan River valley. Not at all auspicious for Canada's 116th birthday and Diana's 22nd.

But if you don't believe in magic, you might well have changed your mind at Edmonton's Commonwealth Stadium that afternoon. For just as the white convertible, carrying the Prince and his young wife, rolled onto the track, and the 60,000 spectators cheered in welcome, the sun broke through, charging all who saw it with a wondrous elation.

Then it all began. The pageantry of Universiade '83 was underway. The opening ceremonies of the fourth largest annual sporting event in the world were highlighted by giant balloons inflated over a map of Canada, the size of a football field, a fly-past of the Canadian Snowbirds and a folklore performance boasting 3,000 dancers in the centre field.

As the 4,500 athletes paraded around the track, healthy and smiling, at the prime of their physical lives, they were acknowledged by the Prince and Princess. Argentines swung by at the top of the alphabetical list, smiling and clicking their cameras for pictures of the Prince and Princess of Wales. The heir to the British throne gave them a nod in return. There were other ironic moments. As the teams marched in alphabetical order, the United States and the USSR found themselves in tandem, and when the teams lined up in the field after

ABOVE: *TRH, in period costume, tour Fort Edmonton before a "Klondike Days" barbecue.*

FACING PAGE, ABOVE: *A highland piper regales costumed guests before the barbecue hosted by the Mayor of Edmonton.*

RIGHT: *Charles sports new badges given to him by athletes in Edmonton.*

FACING PAGE, BELOW: *The pageantry of opening ceremonies of Universiade '83 on Canada Day in Commonwealth Stadium.*

A chuckling Premier Lougheed and the Princess of Wales enjoy a quip from Prince Charles.

Diana waves farewell to Canada before boarding the Canadian Forces jet bound for London, and home.

the parade, Lebanon and Israel found themselves side by side. But the Canadian team, 300 strong, brought the stands to their feet in exuberant applause. When the Maple Leaf flag went up the white flagpole, and the athletes and spectators rose for *O Canada*, it was a moment of tangible emotion and pride, never to be forgotten by any who were there.

In his opening remarks Charles thanked Canadians for their "overflowing" warmth and kindness and was pleased that Diana had "the good sense and excellent taste to be born on Canada's birthday." He summed up their visit by announcing to all that he and his wife had been "spoiled thoroughly" by Canadian hospitality, and he promised to return soon, as long as "you don't get tired of us."

Charles and Diana then stepped into their white convertible to leave for the airport, and on cue from the announcer, everyone in the stadium rose to sing *Happy Birthday* to the Princess of Wales. With that jubilant chorus echoing from the stand, the car circled the track for a last wave from the dazzling Diana and the Prince at her side, and they were gone.

What are a prince and princess for? The London *Times* asked the question and answered it. Obviously, to be seen by as many of their loyal admirers as possible. Judging by the enthusiastic reception they received from young people across the country, and the unexpectedly large crowds, this visit has confirmed the tradition of monarchy in Canada for another generation. And if there had been a closeted republican in the crowd, one direct hit from Diana's dazzling blue eyes would have sent him running for a Royal Standard.

For Charles and Diana prove themselves to be wonderful people, and they make wonderful symbols. They stand for domestic virtues and responsibilities. They stand for fairness and propriety. They stand for tradition and the shared values of the Commonwealth. In this fast changing world, not many things, at a glance, seem worth keeping. The Crown will remain a sparkling living institution as its responsibilities are gradually taken over by this young and handsome couple.

ACKNOWLEDGEMENTS

Norm Betts, Canada Wide: centre opening (left); centre opening (right); centrefold; centre, far right (above); p. 18 (top); p.19 (top); p. 26 (top). Government of Canada: p. 19 (bottom right). Tim Graham: p. 5 (left) (topright); p. 7 (bottom). Justin Hall: p. 23; p. 24 (top) (bottom); p. 25 (top); p. 26 (bottom). Anwar Hussein: p. 6 (top) (bottom). Keystone Press: p. 4 (above); p. 7 (top). Miller Services: p. 2 (lower right). Press Association: p. 4 (right). John Reeves: p. 9; p. 11 (bottom); p. 12 (bottom); p. 13 (bottom); p. 14; p. 15 (bottom right); p. 16 (bottom). Rex Features: p. 5 (bottom right). John Rodgers: front and back covers; p. 1; p. 8; p. 11 (top); p. 12 (top); p. 15 (top) (bottom left); p. 16 (top); centre, facing p. 16; centre, far left (above); centre, far left (below); centre, far right (below); centre, facing p. 17 (top left); centre, facing p. 17 (top right); centre, facing p. 17 (mid-right); centre, facing p. 17 (bottom right); p. 20 (left) (top right) (bottom); p. 21 (bottom); p. 25 (bottom); p. 27 (top) (bottom); p. 28 (top) (bottom); p. 29 (left) (right) p. 30 (top) (bottom); p. 31 (top) (bottom); p. 32 (left) (right). Paul Russell: p. 10 (top) (bottom); centre, facing p. 17 (mid-left); centre, facing p. 17 (bottom left); p. 17; p. 21 (top left); p. 22. Royal Windsor Library, reproduced by gracious permission of Her Majesty The Queen: p. 2 (lower left). Fred Wardle: p. 18 (bottom); p. 19 (bottom left); p. 21 (top right).